ICE CREAM

THE FULL SCOOP

BY **GAIL GIBBONS**

Holiday House / New York

To Ariana

Special thanks to Jon F. Snyder, who owns the ice-cream
company Il Laboratorio del Gelato in New York City.

Copyright © 2006 by Gail Gibbons
All Rights Reserved
Printed and Bound in March 2023 at Toppan Leefung, DongGuan City, China.
www.holidayhouse.com
12 14 16 18 20 19 17 15 13
Library of Congress Cataloging-in-Publication Data
Gibbons, Gail.
Ice cream : the full scoop / by Gail Gibbons.
p. cm.
ISBN-13: 978-0-8234-2000-1 (hardcover)
ISBN-10: 0-8234-2000-0 (hardcover)
1. Ice cream, ices, etc.—Juvenile literature.
2. Ice cream, ices, etc.—History—Juvenile literature.
I. Title.
TX795.G53 2006
641.8'62—dc22
2005052575
ISBN-13: 978-0-8234-2155-8 (paperback)

ICE-CREAM SCOOP

CONES

Ice-cream cones. Ice-cream bars. Ice-cream sodas. Ice cream is a frozen treat made mostly of cream, milk, sugar, and flavorings. Almost every-one loves to eat sweet, cold ice cream.

No one really knows how or when the first ice cream was made. Some believe that people mixed snow, milk, and rice together in China about 3,000 years ago.

About 700 years ago a famous Italian trader, Marco Polo, came home from China bringing recipes for flavored ices. Chefs for European royalty experimented with new combinations of icy treats. Finally cream was added, and there was a new dessert we now call "ice cream."

About 300 years ago the British brought ice-cream recipes to the American colonies. Ice cream was made by shaking the icy mixture in a special pan for a long time. Only the wealthy were served ice cream because it was so difficult to get ice to make it.

About 250 years ago some Americans started harvesting ice from ponds and lakes in the winter. It was stored in icehouses and also shipped to the South. Now people could make ice cream year round. It was served only at special events.

THE ICE-CREAM MAKER

ICE CHIPS were placed in the OUTSIDE CHAMBER.

SALT was added to the ice to make it melt into SLUSH.

OUTSIDE CHAMBER

INSIDE CHAMBER

The ICE-CREAM MIXTURE was poured into the INSIDE CHAMBER.

An ICE-CREAM MIXTURE was made up of cream, sugar or honey, and flavoring, such as strawberries or peaches.

In 1841 a woman from New Jersey named Nancy Johnson invented the hand-cranked ice-cream maker, also called an ice-cream freezer. Now ice cream could be made a lot faster just by turning a crank.

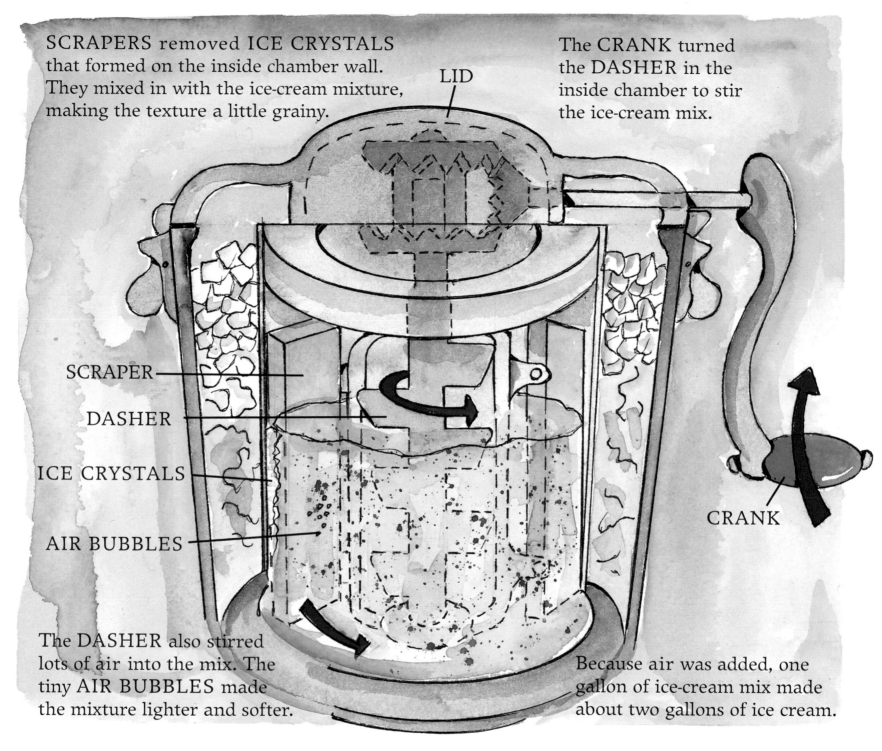

SCRAPERS removed ICE CRYSTALS that formed on the inside chamber wall. They mixed in with the ice-cream mixture, making the texture a little grainy.

The CRANK turned the DASHER in the inside chamber to stir the ice-cream mix.

LID

SCRAPER

DASHER

ICE CRYSTALS

AIR BUBBLES

CRANK

The DASHER also stirred lots of air into the mix. The tiny AIR BUBBLES made the mixture lighter and softer.

Because air was added, one gallon of ice-cream mix made about two gallons of ice cream.

The ice-cream maker became very popular. It took only one hour to churn the ice-cream mixture into creamy ice cream.

Two of the earliest flavorings for ice cream were vanilla and chocolate. Vanilla flavoring was made from powdered vanilla beans. Chocolate flavoring was made from powdered cocoa beans.

Throughout the 1800s people held ice-cream socials. This became a popular way to entertain friends. Everyone took turns cranking the ice-cream maker. Then they shared the ice cream.

Some people still enjoy using ice-cream makers to make their favorite ice cream.

To the ice-cream mix, people added blueberries, raspberries, maple syrup . . . for whatever flavor they wanted.

THE ICE-CREAM BUSINESS

PUMP LINE

CUP

MILK LINE

Cows. It all still begins at the dairy farm. The cows are milked twice a day. Some cows, such as Jersey cows, give creamier milk than others.

The milk is kept at about 40° Fahrenheit (4° Celsius).

PIPELINE

COOLING TANK

The milk is piped to a cooling tank. The milk is kept cool so it won't spoil.

A truck comes to the dairy farm. The milk is pumped into the tank of the truck, where it is still kept cool.

The milk is delivered to the ice-cream factory. Other trucks are there too. Some hold liquid sugar. Other trucks deliver many products that make up the different flavors of ice cream.

At the factory the milk is put into a separator. This is where the cream and milk are separated from each other.

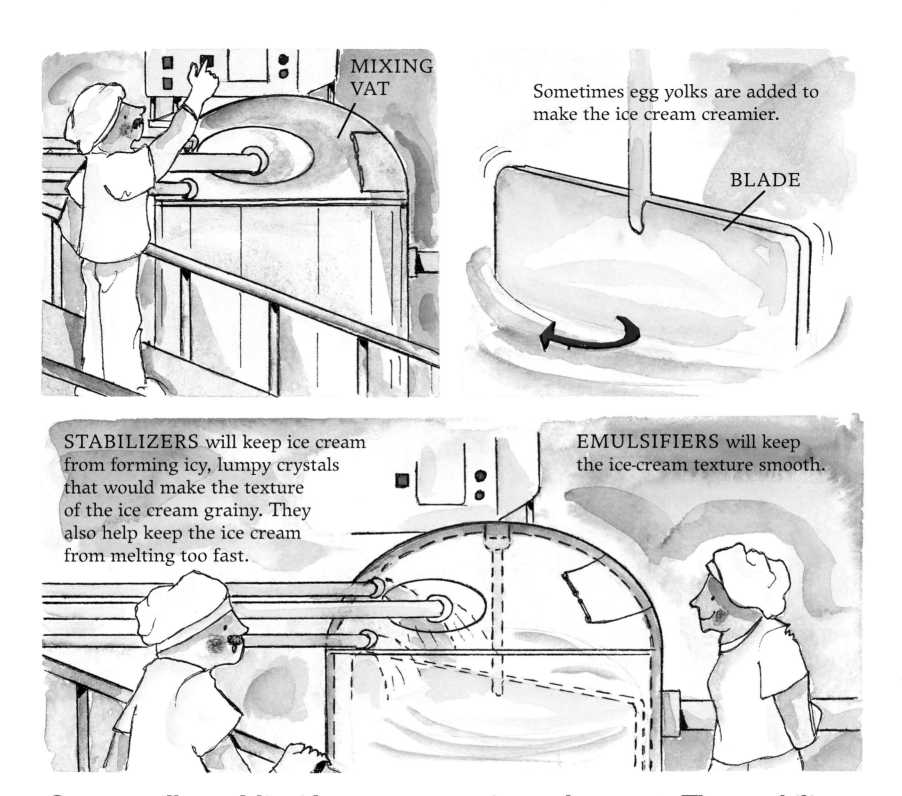

MIXING VAT

Sometimes egg yolks are added to make the ice cream creamier.

BLADE

STABILIZERS will keep ice cream from forming icy, lumpy crystals that would make the texture of the ice cream grainy. They also help keep the ice cream from melting too fast.

EMULSIFIERS will keep the ice-cream texture smooth.

Cream, milk, and liquid sugar are put into a large vat. Then stabilizers and emulsifiers are added. All these ingredients are mixed together.

PASTEURIZER

BACTERIA
may cause disease.

TOUR

LOUIS PASTEUR
invented pasteurization
in the 1860s.

Then the mixture is put in a pasteurizer. Here the mix is heated to kill any harmful bacteria. This is called pasteurization. The temperature inside the pasteurizer gets up to about 170° Fahrenheit (77° Celsius).

Next the mixture flows into a homogenizer, which breaks down any small particles of butterfat. The homogenizer forces the mix through tiny valves under high pressure, which makes the mixture smooth.

COOLER

Now it is time for the mix to be cooled. It is moved to a cooler and stays there for a few hours. The temperature inside the cooler is about 40° Fahrenheit (4° Celsius), which makes the mixture firmer.

Then the thick mixture is pumped into a freezer. Inside the freezer, blades spin around, forcing air into the ice-cream mix, making it softer and smoother. The mixture expands as the air is pumped into it.

Now the ice cream goes to different vats for flavoring. There is vanilla, chocolate, mint, and many other flavors. Often fruits, nuts, raisins, or other foods are added to make different flavors and kinds of ice creams. Now we have ice cream that is very similar to the ice cream made in the first ice-cream makers.

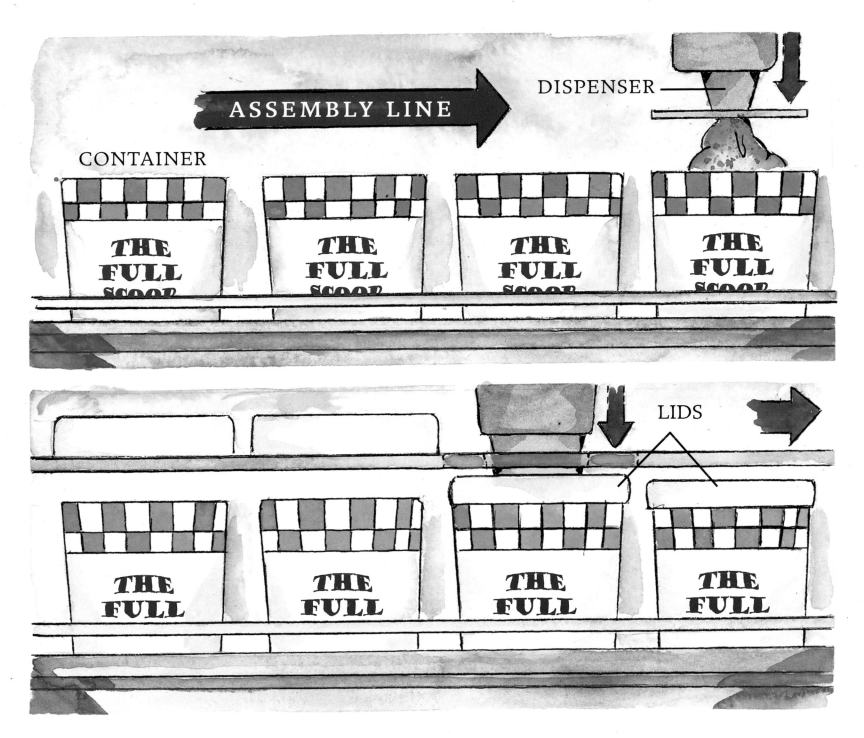

The different-flavored ice creams are sent to their packaging areas. Then containers move along an assembly line. When each container stops, a dispenser fills it up and packs it down with soft, tasty ice cream.

The packaged ice cream is moved to a freezer room. Inside the room it is very cold, about –20° Fahrenheit (–29° Celsius). The ice cream becomes hard and firm.

It is time for the ice cream to be shipped to stores or other places where it will be sold to customers. The ice cream is moved onto refrigerated trucks that are very cold inside.

People buy ice cream at so many different places. Some people order ice cream in restaurants and buy it at ice-cream stands. There are ice-cream trucks and carts too.

THREE COMMON CONTAINERS

HALF GALLON
1.89 liters

QUART
.95 liter

PINT
.47 liter

Most people buy ice cream at their grocery store. Ice cream can be sold in many different containers. It is available without sugar too.

In 1904, at the St. Louis World's Fair, an ice-cream vendor ran out of paper cups to scoop ice cream into. A waffle maker in the next booth offered him some of his waffles.

A VENDOR is someone who sells something.

The ice-cream vendor rolled a waffle into a cone shape and put a scoop of ice cream in it. It was the beginning of the ice-cream cone.

An ICE-CREAM SANDWICH is ice cream between two cookies.

An ICE-CREAM SODA is ice cream scooped into soda water.

A BANANA SPLIT is a banana cut in half with scoops of ice cream on top and a flavored syrup poured on top.

An ICE-CREAM SUNDAE is scoops of ice cream covered with chocolate syrup, caramel sauce, or other kinds of toppings.

An ICE-CREAM BAR is a bar of ice cream with a coating on it. Usually it has a wooden stick in it so it can be held.

PIE À LA MODE is a scoop of ice cream served with a slice of pie.

An ICE-CREAM CAKE is a special dessert served for special occasions. It is ice cream formed to look like a cake.

Ice cream can be enjoyed as many different treats.

There are all kinds of ways to eat ice cream!

Vanilla is the most popular flavor of ice cream. Chocolate ice cream is the second favorite flavor.

Grocery stores didn't start selling ice cream until the 1930s.

When hot chocolate syrup is poured over ice cream, it is called a hot fudge sundae.

In 1920 a man named Harry Burt started serving a chocolate-coated ice-cream bar on a wooden stick to be used as a handle. He named it the Good Humor Bar.

Some people like having sprinkles or chocolate drops and other things put on their ice cream.

Americans eat a lot of ice cream; annual consumption averages about 15 quarts (14.2 liters) per person.

Almost 10 percent of all milk produced by cows in the United States and Canada is used to make ice cream.

ICE-CREAM SUNDAYS were first served as a special treat on Sundays. The spelling was changed to ICE-CREAM SUNDAES when people started eating them on different days of the week.

More ice cream is sold on Sunday than on any other day of the week.

Ice cream is a treat . . . but DON'T EAT TOO MUCH!